A NOVEL BY MEENAKSHI SINGH

# INSIDE THE NIRBHAYA RAPE

AFTERMATH

*BEYOND THE HEADLINES - A DEEP DIVE IN THE NIRBHAYA CASE*

© **Meenakshi Singh 2023**

**All rights reserved**

All rights reserved by author. No part of this publication may be reproduced, stored in a retrieval system or transmitted in any form or by any means, electronic, mechanical, photocopying, recording or otherwise, without the prior permission of the author.

Although every precaution has been taken to verify the accuracy of the information contained herein, the author and publisher assume no responsibility for any errors or omissions. No liability is assumed for damages that may result from the use of information contained within.

First Published in April 2023

**ISBN: 978-93-5741-298-8**

**BLUEROSE PUBLISHERS**

www.BlueRoseONE.com
info@bluerosepublishers.com
+91 8882 898 898

**Cover Design:**
Muskan Sachdeva

**Typographic Design:**
Pooja Sharma

**Distributed by:** BlueRose, Amazon, Flipkart

# Contents

Chapter 1: Disastrous Night Of 16th December, 2012 ...... 1

Chapter 2: Investigation Go On ......................................... 4

Chapter 3: Nirbhaya's Last Word To Her Parents ............ 6

Chapter 4: Turning Tables In Lives Of Nirbhaya's Criminals ...................................................................... 8

Chapter 5: Hearing Goes On ........................................... 9

Chapter 6: Finally Rapists Are Hanged !! ....................... 11

Chapter 7: Years After Nirbhaya : Perceptions And Criticisms ...................................................................... 13

Chapter 8: Changes In Rape Laws, Criticisms And Perceptions ................................................................... 15

Chapter 9: Effectiveness Of Laws, Unaddressed Questions ...................................................................... 21

Chapter 10: Independent Judiciary, Criticisms, Effectiveness ................................................................. 24

Chapter 11: My Words To Audience ............................. 27

Chapter 12: Nirbhaya's Mom's Message ........................ 29

## *Chapter 1*

# Disastrous Night Of 16th December, 2012

It was a cold, night on 16 December 2012 when a girl named Jyoti Singh ( nirbhaya) gets brutally gang-raped in a moving bus by six men.

Nirbhaya gang rape is not just a crime, it is insanity, a shameful tragedy that should the whole world and made the country's blood boil, leading to protests, and anger, not only national but international also.

The roads were full of public protests, and the area of munirka still gives expressions of horror and brutality.

**Public protests were going on against the state and central government for failing to provide adequate security for women.**

Once upon a time, there was a 22-year-old hardworking physiotherapy intern, who loved her life, parents, and friends. On one normal night of 16 December 2012, she and her friend were returning home after watching the film "life of pie" at PVR select city walk, Saket, south Delhi. Though they were unable to find any auto, for Dwarka. They boarded the bus at Munirka for Dwarka at about 9.30 pm (IST). There were six men on the bus including the driver. One of the men, identified as a minor, called them in a strange voice saying " Dwarka Dwarka. Later nirbhaya's friend became suspicious when the bus driver changed their route. After that they got engaged in a serious argument with the conductor present there, asking why they were alone at such a late hour.

They are in anger seeing Nirbhaya and her friend laughing and talking.

During the argument, the five men beat her friend and dragged them to the back of the bus, the moment he fell unconscious after being beaten with an iron rod. One of the men then dragged Jyoti to the end of the bus, beating her with a rod and raping her while the bus driver continued to drive. All five were continuously raping nirbhaya, beating her with an iron rod.

But the question is, is that just rape?

No, it was an inhumane, barbaric, shameful act that started when the driver went back, took an iron rod, and inserted it into the victim. They didn't end it like that but crossed all the limits of insanity by inserting their hands and pulling out her intestines, ripping them apart from her vagina. After those monsters are done with the rape, they throw both victims from the moving bus. Around 11 pm, the passerby called the Delhi police, from where they both were taken to Safdarjung hospital where they were given emergency treatment and placed on ventilation.

The body was covered with blood, with countless cuts on the face, and bite marks all over her body.

**Doctors were amazed after seeing Nirbhaya's condition, they said they have never seen this brutality in their long years of service.**

It is because of an iron rod that caused massive damage to her genitals, uterus, and intestines. Intestines were seen to be hanging out of the vagina and rectum. The only words Nirbhaya can utter are " Don't tell anything to my father " ( मेरे पापा को कुछ मत बताना).

## Chapter 2

# Investigation Go On

The investigation was started when south Delhi deputy police commissioner Chhaya Sharma received a call after 2. Am on December 16, 2012. Not having proper information about the case, she was disturbed and went to the hospital after she shattered and decided to catch all the suspects as soon as possible. She was surprised to know that the incident took place in a moving bus at 9.30- 10.30 pm on a well-lit road in Delhi. The investigation process was so difficult, with no witnesses, except the victims of a horrific crime.

**DCP Chhaya Sharma came up with the most experienced investigation team launching a multistate manhunt.**

With criticism, and pressure from the media, and people, the Delhi police worked hard, to end the investigation within five days, catching all the criminals, and leaving no question over their conduct. Teamwork and diligence followed up in the process when Delhi police were successfully able to get the bus within 18 hours, sending it for verification where the forensic team came across various disturbing objects like - an iron rod, screwdriver, a piece of cloth, intestines, and blood all over the bus. This evidence helped Chhaya Sharma and her team to get a clear idea of the horrific scene.

With years of experience, Chhaya Sharma has learned not to get carried away with emotions dealing with all protests patiently.

Protests were seen in all major parts of Delhi, be it India Gate, redfort, hauz khas, or munirka. Even outside Vasant vihar police station and Safdarjung hospital, the south district officers handled protestors, media, and politicians with great credibility.

# Chapter 3

# Nirbhaya's Last Word To Her Parents

With all her strength and anger in her eyes, Nirbhaya gave a four-page statement in Hindi to the magistrate five days after the barbaric attack on her. On 19th December 2012, she underwent her fifth surgery in which most of her remaining intestine was removed. On 21 December, a committee of doctors was appointed to plan the best medical care for her. Today she scribbled on a piece of paper - "mother, I want to live".

On 25th December, she was in critical condition, and it was decided to take her to Mount Elizabeth hospital in Singapore for further care. During the 6-hour flight, she suffered from - " cardiac arrest ".

On 28th December her condition was critical as she suffered brain damage, pneumonia, and abdominal infection-fighting for her life.

She said, " I want to see them burnt alive ".

(में नहीं चाहती ये दुबारा किसी लड़की के साथ हो)।

Her condition continued to deteriorate, and she died at 4.45 am on 29th December. She always acts as if she is fine in front of her parents, and lastly talks to her brother saying - " मम्मी पापा का ध्यान रखना"!

Her body was then cremated on 30th December in Delhi under high police security.

## Chapter 4

# Turning Tables In Lives Of Nirbhaya's Criminals

As per recordings of CCTV cameras, on highways, description of bus, and sketches of assailants with the help of male victims, six men were arrested, in connection with heinous crime. They were 30 yr old ram Singh ( bus driver) and 26 yr old brother, mukesh Singh. 20 yr old vinay Sharma ( gym instructor), 19 yr old pawan Gupta, and 17 yr old juvenile namely Mohammad afroz from Uttar Pradesh.

**All the accused were arrested and charged with sexual assault and murder .**

## Chapter 5

# Hearing Goes On

As all rapists of Nirbhaya were caught there's still one issue setting up the fire. The juvenile Mohammad Alfroz, the name was later changed to Raju in the middle due to his age being 17 yrs and 6 months old on the day of the crime. But on 28 Jan 2013, the juvenile justice board determined he was a juvenile and should not be tried as an adult. The minor was tried separately in juvenile court.

**Caption - It was seen that the Janata party was highly supporting the prosecution of minors as adults because of the violent nature and assault he did with nirbhaya.**

After that hearing was scheduled on 25 July then for 5 and then for 19 August.

On 31 August, he was convicted of rape and murder by the juvenile justice board and given 3 yrs of imprisonment, spending 8 months in remand during the trial. He was then released on 20 Dec 2015. After his release, his family refused to accept him. The government afterward provided him with the machine and he was working as a cook.

On 5 May supreme court rejected the convict's appeal considering the seriousness of the barbaric crime that had shaken the whole nation. Though our constitution offers legal rights to convicts they can have the right to file review petitions. On 9 July 2018, the Supreme Court rejected the review petition by three convicts.

In Nov 2019, the Supreme Court dismissed the review petition from Akshay requesting mercy.

## Chapter 6

# Finally Rapists Are Hanged !!

Defence lawyer Akshay told the Supreme Court to appeal to the president. In January 2020, a 5 judge bench of the Supreme Court rejected the petitions of convicts. On 17 January 2020, a death warrant was issued for the nirbhaya rapists by the Delhi court, with an estimated date of 22 January 2020 at 7:00 am in Tihar jail.

On 17 Feb 3rd a death warrant was issued with the execution date of 3 march. Though there were numerous pleas and appeals by families of convicts to stay on death sentence, however, the date for execution remained the same.

**The biggest question was even after brutal assault what stopped an independent judiciary to take quick steps against these monsters?**

**Government authorities and the victim's mother alleged that four convicts were intentionally irritating them by filing petitions again and again as they are aware of their legal rights. They are disturbing the legal process, causing delays in their execution.**

On 4 march 2020, 4 death warrants were issued with an execution date of 20 march 2020 at 5:30 am.

Finally, the day was here when all the convicts were shivering afraid of their news of hanging. On 20 March, at 5:30 am they were executed at Tihar jail. They were hanged on gallows specially designed for four people.

**Caption - It was not just hanging, it was the victory of a mother who turned into a" rebel ", an " activist " for her daughter, who faced those monsters for continuous 45 minutes, underwent that pain, and cried that night but no one heard.**

"Late but got justice," says Nirbhaya's mother to the judiciary. She believes her daughter rests in peace now. Moreover, it will be a lesson and warning for other rapists and an assurance to all women that " No women will be seen in this brutal situation again ".

## Chapter 7

# Years After Nirbhaya : Perceptions And Criticisms

Even after 10 years have passed, the streets of Delhi are haunted by the brutal rape of 25 yr old women physiotherapist who boarded a bus in south Delhi with her friend. The horrific Nirbhaya rape of 2012 is a definitive milestone. It shocked the nation with such force that lawmakers rushed to strengthen laws and put in place systems and infrastructure to ensure such insanity never repeated. However, according to the national crime records bureau statistics it was stated more than 2780 lakhs crime against women including - trafficking, rape, harassment, kidnapping.

**How safe are women in India? The government may be pressing ahead with women focused issues, but the latest data by NCRB offer a reality check.**

Today while writing this book, my hands are shivering, my heart is heavy with all that pain I felt when I was 8 yr old, heard about nirbhaya rape case. I saw my parents were crying on her death, no doubt the whole india cried for her. Just because a few cases hit the headlines or make an impact on social media that doesn't mean we should ignore most of the brutal cases which have left traces in our mind.

Some of the most brutal cases were -

19 yr old girl brutally gang raped and murdered on Feb 2012, after being allegedly abducted by 3 men in Dwarka. We can't even imagine the cruelty, brutality with which she was killed. The depressing thing is how those 3 monsters get easy bail. The other case was in 2018, when eight yr old nomadic girl was brutally raped for four days before being killed in barbaric manner. It was shocking after finding out about the accused - Temple priest, police officer, sub inspector. Seriously, the one on whom we believe are themselves committing these horrifying crimes?

Nothing makes me ashamed to criticise a country like Delhi where small girls become soft targets to satisfy the lust of these monsters. The place of rape was temple the place where we worship lakshmimata, our daughters are allegedly raped.

## Chapter 8

# Changes In Rape Laws, Criticisms And Perceptions

The calls for justice were loud in the days after the Nirbhaya gang rape. People all over the world are demanding that rapists be hanged. When it was reported that the most violent of her rapists was the minor boy, there was outrage over the fact that he would be out in just three years as a minor cannot be tried or sentenced as an adult.

**In 2013, the criminal law amendment act made several changes to Indian rape and sexual crime laws and investigation procedures, the principal among them being broadened definitions of rape and severe punishment for it.**

Here are some important IPCs related to sexual crimes committed by anyone.

- **Section 375**

    Section 375 of the Indian penal code (IPC) was amended to broaden the definition of rape from penile penetration to penetration by other means as well. Such as orally or by hand or any other object. A man is said to commit " rape" if he inserts to any extent, any object or part of the body, not being a penis, into the vagina, the urethra, or the anus of a woman or makes her do so with him or any other person, or manipulates any part of the body of a woman to cause penetration applies his mouth to vagina, anus, urethra of a woman or makes her do so with him or any other person. The age of consent was also set at 18 years.

- **Section 376**

    Section 376 was also amended to increase punishment for rape under the amended section, rape was made punishable by a minimum of 7 yrs imprisonment further amended to 10 yrs rape causing death or vegetative state was made punishable by a minimum of 20 years.

    **Some of the other amendments to IPCs given below -**

    **Section 166(A)**

    It was inserted, which punishes police officers for disobeying lawful instructions and not doing their mandatory duty as per law with imprisonment of 6-24 months.

    **Section 166(B)**

    It was inserted, which punishes denial of treatment to victims at the hospital and not informing police of an alleged offense with imprisonment for one year or fine, or both.

Section 326 (A) and (B) are introduced to deal with acid attacks and attempts of acid attacks, punishable by imprisonment for not less than 10 years extendable to life imprisonment.

### Section 354(A)

It was inserted which punished sexual harassment through unwelcome physical contact, request, or demand involving pornography with imprisonment extendable to 3 years and sexual harassment through sexual comments with imprisonment up to one year

### Section 354(C)

It made voyeurism punishable by a minimum of one year. It means to watch or take photos or videos of women in private acts without their consent.

### Section 354(D)

Made stalking punishable with three years of imprisonment for a first conviction and 5 yrs of conviction.

## Other important amendments

- **Marital Rape laws**

Martial rape is defined as the act of forcing your partner into having a sexual relationship without proper consent.

This is an act of disrespecting a woman's decision, against her will, outraging modesty.

According to IPC 375, it includes all forms of sexual assaults involving non-consensual intercourse with women.

**Here are some important recommendations which support that marital rape should be criminalized and considered as " Rape".**

-According to the protection of women from domestic violence act, of 2005

Any violence including physical, sexual, and verbal is punishable.

**-UN committee - Indian judiciary should criminalize " Marital rape".**

- **J.S Verma committee**

    After the 16 Dec 2012 gang rape recommended the same.

**India is one of the 34 countries that have decriminalised marital rape.**

**The exploitation of following rights of women suggested that there is a need for proper law regarding marital rapes -**

- **Article 14** Right to equality
- **Article 15** prohibits discrimination based on sex, caste, etc
- **Article 19(1)** Freedom of speech and expression
- **Article 21** Right to life

**K.S puttaswamy VS Union of India 2017 also supported the decision to criminalise marital rapes based on four crucial aspects-**

- Decision autonomy
- Bodily integrity
- Individual freedom
- Dignity
- **Ban on two-finger test**

Supreme Court has declared that any person conducting the " **Two finger test** " on rape or sexual assault survivors will be found guilty of misconduct. The court has declared the test as " regressive " with no scientific or relevant meaning. According to the explanation, it is said that during the 2 finger test, the victim has to go under trauma and feeling of assault once again. There are many other options to test rapecases.

**In 2013 too, in Lilly v. State of Haryana,** the supreme court held two-finger test violates the right of rape survivors.

Section 53A of the evidence act states that previous sexual experience shall not be relevant to the issue of consent or quality of consent, in prosecutions of sexual offences.

It is also directed that health providers should conduct proper, safe medical detailed examinations of victims which should not lead to pressuring them or any other misconceptions or illogical questions related to their previous sexual relationships. In the case of sexual assault, it is the prime duty of the doctor to monitor the marks and signs of recent intercourse. Therefore it is undesirable to conduct two-finger tests on a victim, which has no evidential cruciality in the investigation.

Secondly, police departments and forensic science laboratories should work in the proper way to understand the sensitivity of rape cases.

There are many areas in which two-finger tests are still conducted which can be only stopped with effective implementation and a holistic approach toward rape victims' rights. An institutional mechanism is the need of the hour now in addition to the roles and responsibilities of police personnel and other members included in rape cases.

## Chapter 9

# Effectiveness Of Laws, Unaddressed Questions

Following the shock and outrage over the 2012 Delhi gang rape, the congress-led union government formed a three-member panel led by Justice JS Verma, former Chief Justice of the Supreme Court.

It was known as the justice Verma committee. While some recommendations of the Verma panel made it to amendments, some did not, and some resultant amendments were against the recommendations.

While amendments dropped recommendations to penalise marital rape, the amendments introduced death. The penalty was not recommended by the panel.

Though the definition of rape is liberalised, it remained and remains to this day women-centric Moreover, the age of consent was not changed to 16, as the Verma panel had recommended.

The amendments that followed the nirbhaya case were reactionary and fulfilled the " collective conscience " of people who were demanding the death penalty to put rapists out of outrage.

There is the issue of improper enforcement of laws but there is also the issue of a society that continues to be governed by patriarchal nations. It's not just legal but it's also societal. Neither the law nor society can solve issues on its own.

**The death penalty for rapists only remedied the national and international backlash at the time, but did not deter crimes against women over the years.**

Besides the death penalty, it is also crucial to address the issue of the age of consent. The Verma panel recommended it to be set at 16 but amendments set it at 18. As we are aware that it's very natural for sexual relations to be made under the age of 18. Such sex remains criminalised. There needs to be a study to assess the maturity of those under 18s, say 14 to 18 yr old, to see if they are mature enough to understand the concept of consent.

# The juvenile justice Act Amendment

As we are aware the juvenile justice act amendment deals with minors accused and convicted of crimes but was not amended in the immediate aftermath of the 2012 Delhi gang rape, it was amended and it's understood that the amendment was forced by public outrage over the nirbhaya case. One of the rapists in the Nirbhaya case, often said to be the most brutal of all, was a minor while the others were sentenced to death and were eventually executed, the minor was only sent to a reform centre for three and was set free in 2015. Following the outrage, the juvenile justice act often known as the JJ act was amended to enable the trial of the accused aged 16 - 18 years as an adult if accused of " heinous crimes". The decision to try the accused as an adult is taken by the juvenile Justice Board ( JJB), as per the JJ act.

The amended JJ act says " In case of the heinous offence alleged to have been committed by a child who has completed or is above the age of 16 yrs, the board (JJB) shall conduct a preliminary assessment about his mental and physical capacity to commit such offence, ability to understand the consequences of offences and circumstances in which he allegedly committed the offence. Even when juveniles aged 16-18 are convicted as an adult for heinous offences, the juvenile is not sentenced like an adult. For the same offence, an adult could be sentenced to death or life, but a juvenile even when being tried and convicted as an adult is not sentenced to life imprisonment or death.

## Chapter 10

# Independent Judiciary, Criticisms, Effectiveness

As we are aware, an independent judiciary has been ensured by our Indian Constitution. With this independence, the judiciary can safeguard people's rights and freedom, ensuring equal protection for all. For citizens, the judiciary is the only " door to justice ". The effectiveness of the law and the respect people have for the law, the respect that people have for the law and the government which enacts it is dependent upon the judiciary's independence to make fair decisions.

Though there are many complaints related to judgments of the Supreme Court over rape victims. Four years after the supreme court referred to justice J.S Verma's committee's recommendation to make marital rape a crime, under IPC section (375).

Since independence it was ensured that the judiciary will favour the unprivileged half of society, especially women, her evidence cannot be thrown aside. She is entitled to freedom / equal justice.

There should be more consideration given to the gravity of crime rather than the **Benefit of the doubt**. By doing this, we are giving these monsters a chance to show this cruelty again.

Three men in the chhawla case of 2012 have been given bail, as the prosecution had failed to prove charges against the trio " beyond reasonable doubt ".

Other evidence like - the identity of the Indica car, seizures, sealing, collection of medical evidence - DNA, semen evidence in the vagina of the victim, and unnatural sex.

The Supreme Court says this evidence didn't fulfil the fact that these rapists should be punished.

### Who is faulty here?

The Supreme Court stated that there were lapses in the investigation and trial of the prosecution's case had rested on circumstantial evidence and had failed to prove charges beyond a reasonable doubt.

There was tampering with evidence, material witnesses were also not examined instantly.

49 witnesses, 10 were not cross-examined in the trial. Many others are not adequately cross-examined by defence counsel.

Why were these rapists given these legal rights? And not the victim, why is she always being questioned about her clothes, and at what time she has gone out?

With whom she was travelling?

And still, people dare to ask " Why are our laws more tilted toward women "?

In the legal world, no one is guilty until proven guilty. Similarly, no one is guilty until the court of law declares them so.

There should be no doubt whether the accused is guilty or not. If there is the slightest doubt, no matter how small it is, the benefit will go to the accused.

Law is not sufficient to get rid of any heinous crimes. Law implementation also has limitations.

What is ethical is not always legal, and what is legal is not always ethical.

## Chapter 11

# My Words To Audience

---

Years have passed, and laws are changed, but the question rises " Are the streets of Delhi safe for women "?

Why can't we walk on the streets without being harassed, can't travel in the metro or buses without a group of men staring at us? Much like in 2012, the nirbhaya gang rape and brutality on an eight-year-old girl in kathua shocked the country which shows the national capital remains as unsafe for women as ever.

Though Delhi has reached the top spot for most rape cases.

It is the capital where some illiterate group of men dares to ask a TV reporter " chalti kya" while she was live reporting.

They think that they own the city, they think when women are out in public they should be treated as "public property ". Anyone has the authority to touch her, assault her, rape her, and whatnot.

No one can understand the pain she goes through when they face this insanity and cruelty.

I was in tears, in pain while writing this, reading the statements made by one of the rapists of nirbhaya - Mukesh Singh - "A girl is far more responsible for rape than a boy. A decent girl won't roam around at 9 o'clock She shouldn't fight back and allows the rape. "

No, we don't deserve this, we are equally contributing to the nation for its upliftment.

Is the nation doing anything for our safety?

Rather than keeping brutal rape cases pending for 7-8 years.

Just because of this, people are not ready to let their daughters out at night, where the question arises " when will this stop"?

When will this process of judging them by clothes end?

**Delhi is not the problem, but the people with horrible mentality are!**

**Every day, I wished for something which makes us believe in letting our daughters live in Delhi.**

## Chapter 12

# Nirbhaya's Mom's Message

मुझे अपनी बेटी की दर्दनाक मौत का बहुत अफ़सोस है !

मेरी लड़ाई सिर्फ़ मेरी बेटी के लिये नहीं बल्कि उन सब के लिए है , जिनके साथ ऐसी घटनाएं होती हैं , पर इंसाफ नहीं मिलता .

आज मैं हर लड़की को सचेत करना चाहतीं हूं की अपने आस पास के लोगों से जान पहचानकर संबंध वा बात करे .

आप पढ़िए, लिखिए, आगे बढ़ीये आपका भी हक है .

पर किसी को इतना अधिकार मत दिजिए की वो आपकी इज्जत पर उंगली उठाए.

मेरी बेटी तो वापस नहीं आ सकती , पर हर लड़की निर्भया बनकर बिना डरे अपनी ज़िंदगी जी सकती हैं.

www.ingramcontent.com/pod-product-compliance
Lightning Source LLC
LaVergne TN
LVHW061343080526
838199LV00093B/7181